CW01216421

Lowen

A to Z of Ocean Life

Quarto is the authority on a wide range of topics.
Quarto educates, entertains and enriches the lives of our readers—enthusiasts and lovers of hands-on living.
www.quartoknows.com

Design and editorial: Evolution Design & Digital Ltd (Kent)

Copyright © 2020 Quarto Publishing plc

This edition first published in 2020 by QED Publishing,
an imprint of The Quarto Group.
The Old Brewery, 6 Blundell Street,
London N7 9BH, United Kingdom.
T (0)20 7700 6700 F (0)20 7700 8066
www.QuartoKnows.com

All rights reserved. No part of this publication may be reproduced, stored in a retrieval system, or transmitted in any form or by any means, electronic, mechanical, photocopying, recording, or otherwise, without the prior permission of the publisher, nor be otherwise circulated in any form of binding or cover other than that in which it is published and without a similar condition being imposed on the subsequent purchaser.

A catalogue record for this book is available from the British Library.

ISBN 978-0-7112-5686-6

Manufactured in Guangdong, China CC042020

9 8 7 6 5 4 3 2 1

A to Z OF OCEAN LIFE

QED

Contents

WHAT ARE OCEANS?		6
THE WORLD OCEAN		8
EXPLORING THE OCEAN		10
A	Albatross	12
	American Horseshoe Crab	13
	Anemone	14
	Anglerfish	15
B	Blue Whale	17
	Bull Shark	18
	Butterfly Fish	19
C	Crown of Thorns Starfish	20
	Crustacean	21
CORAL REEFS		22
D	Diatom	24
	Dog Whelk	25
	Dolphin	27
DEEP, DARK SEA		28
E	Echinoderm	30
	Eel	31
	Emperor Penguin	33
F	Fangtooth Fish	34
	Feather Star	35
	Flying Fish	35
FISH		36
G	Garibaldi	38
	Giant Clam	39
	Giant Tube Worm	39
H	Hammerhead Shark	40
	Humpback Whale	41
I	Irukandji Jellyfish	42
	Isopod	43
INVERTEBRATES		44
J	Jackass Penguin	46
	Japanese Spider Crab	47
	Jellyfish	48
K	Kelp	50
	Killer Whale	51
	Kittiwake	52
	Krill	53
L	Leafy Sea Dragon	54
	Leatherback Sea Turtle	55
	Lionfish	56
	Lobster	57
M	Mangrove	58
	Marine Iguana	59
	Mollusc	59

MAMMALS		60
N Narwhal		62
Nautilus		63
O Ocean Sunfish		64
Octopus		65
Otter		66
Oystercatcher		67
OPEN OCEAN		68
P Peacock Mantis Shrimp		70
Polar Bear		71
Portuguese man o' war		71
Puffer Fish		72
PLANTS AND ALGAE		74
POLAR OCEANS		76
Q Queen Angelfish		78
Queen Scallop		79
R Ray		81
Remora Fish		82
Robber Crab		83
REPTILES		84
S Sea Horse		86
Sea Slug		87
Shark		88
SEABIRDS		90
SOS – SAVE OUR SEAS		92
T Tern		94
Tiger Cowrie		95
TIDEs		96
U Upside-Down Jellyfish		98
Urchin		99
V Vampire Squid		100
Vaquita		102
Venus Comb		103
W Walrus		104
Water Monitor		105
Whale Shark		106
Worm		107
X Xanthid Crab		108
X-Ray Tetra		109
Y Yellow-Bellied Sea Snake		110
Yellowfin Tuna		111
Z Zebra Shark		112
Zooplankton		113
Zooxanthellae		113
ZONES		114
GLOSSARY		118

WHAT ARE OCEANS?

Oceans are large, continuous bodies of salt water that cover over 70 per cent of the Earth's surface. They are home to many plants and animals, from tiny fish to giant blue whales.

Animal Homes

An animal's home is called a **habitat**, and the oceans are the world's largest habitat. A crab's habitat is the rocky shore where there are places to hide and lots of snails, urchins and clams to eat. The blue whale's habitat is the open ocean; they are found in every ocean on Earth, except the Arctic.

Why Is the Ocean Salty?

Humans need water to survive, and while oceans make up 97 per cent of all water on Earth, the water in the oceans is too salty to drink! The salt found in the oceans is mostly a result of rainwater. When rain falls, it is slightly acidic and it erodes rocks, picking up small amounts of salt and other minerals. Eventually, that rainwater makes its way to the ocean and causes the seawater to be salty.

North America

Atlantic Ocean

Pacific Ocean

Equator

South America

THE WORLD OCEAN

There are five oceans in the world: the Pacific, Atlantic, Arctic, Indian and Southern Oceans. Together they make one giant ocean, called the World Ocean, and it covers two-thirds of the world's surface.

Southern Ocean

Asia

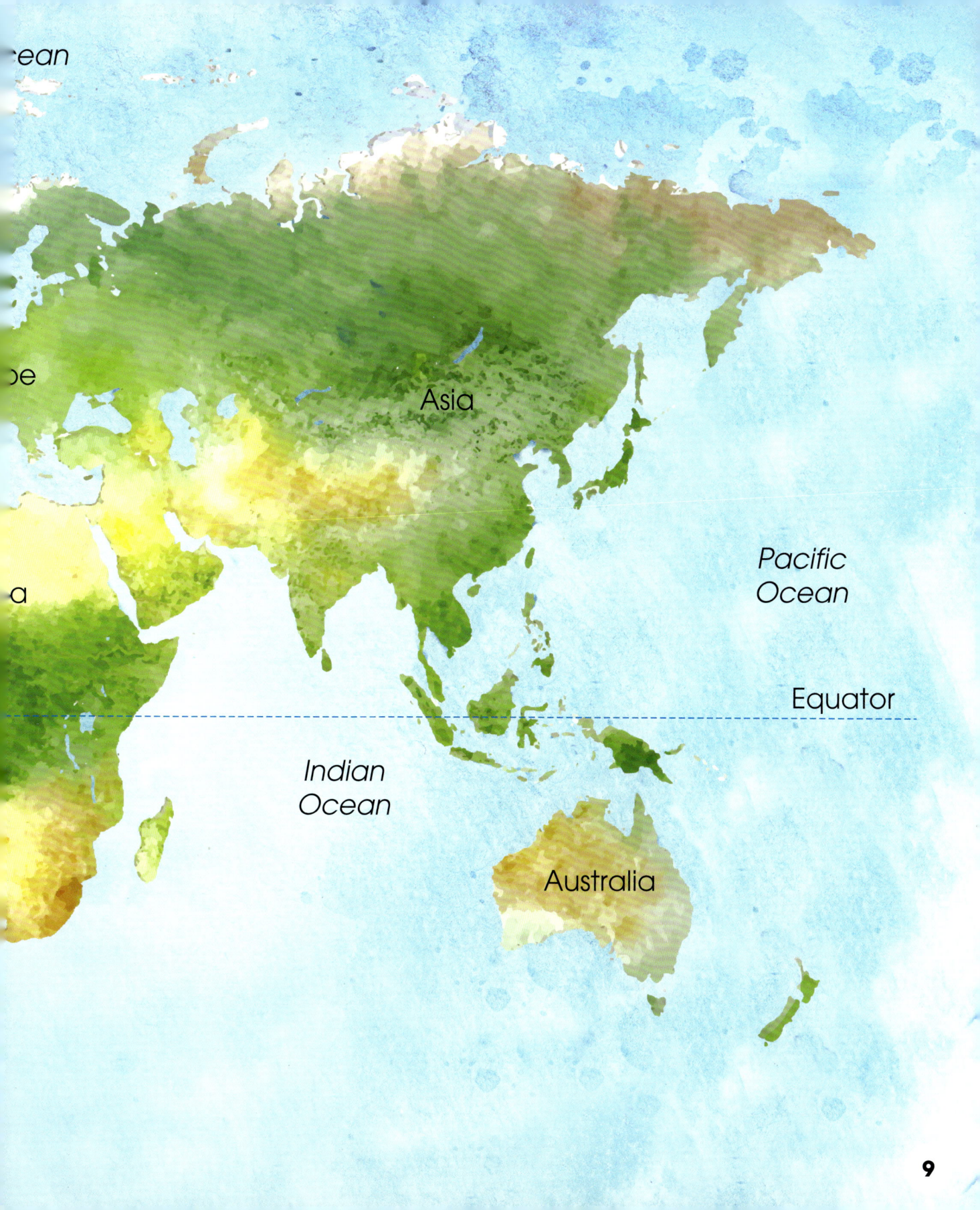

Pacific Ocean

Equator

Indian Ocean

Australia

EXPLORING THE OCEAN

People have explored the oceans for thousands of years, but 95 per cent of the ocean is still a mystery. More people have been to the Moon than have travelled to the deepest part of the Pacific Ocean!

Deep-Sea Expeditions

The only way to learn more about the oceans and the creatures in them is by exploring them. Scientists go on expeditions to make new discoveries and look for unusual or unexpected creatures. They carefully document their findings to help everyone to understand how the ocean is affected by us and how we are affected by the ocean.

Crazy Creatures

Deep-sea expeditions are great for discovering new, interesting **species** of ocean creatures. In a recent month-long expedition off the coast of Australia, scientists uncovered nearly 1000 new species, many of which create their own light through **bioluminescence**!

Drones

In addition to exploring the depths of the ocean, scientists can also learn a lot by observing the ocean's surface. Drones are one way they can film or take photographs of the sea below. This can be very useful for learning about how, where and when animals travel in the ocean.

A

ALBATROSS

Habitat: Islands and coasts

Size: Up to 1.4 metres long

Diet: Fish, jellyfish and crustaceans

These seabirds claim the title of the longest wingspan of any bird – up to 3.4 metres. Albatrosses use their giant wings to catch ocean winds and can glide for hours without flapping their wings. Taking rests by floating on the ocean's surface, these gentle giants will stay at sea for 5 to 10 years before touching down on land.

AMERICAN HORSESHOE CRAB

Habitat: Seabed

Size: Up to 60 centimetres long

Diet: Invertebrates

Despite its name, the American horseshoe crab is more closely related to spiders and scorpions than to crustaceans. It is one of the oldest species on Earth and has been around for more than 300 million years! American horseshoe crabs live along shallow coasts and have ten legs, nine eyes and blue blood that clumps up when it comes in contact with bacteria. Doctors use this unique animal's blood to test whether medical equipment is clean!

A

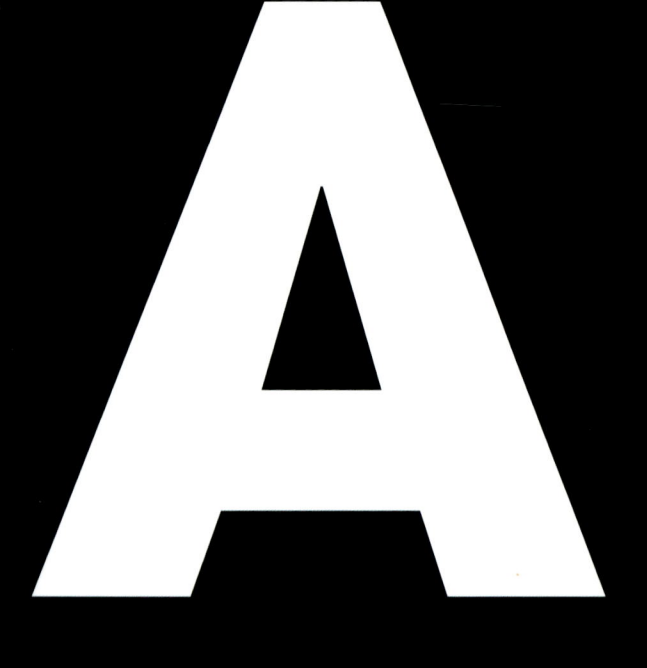

ANEMONE

Habitat: Seabed

Size: From a few millimetres to 1.5 metres wide

Diet: Invertebrates and fish

Anemones may look like plants, but they are actually stinging polyps that spend most of their time attached to rocks or coral reefs. They use their venomous tentacles to catch fish to eat. Clownfish are immune to anemone stings, so they make their homes in its tentacles, which protect the fish from predators.

ANGLERFISH

Habitat: Deep ocean

Size: 5 centimetres to 1 metre long

Diet: Crustaceans and fish

These ugly creatures live in one of the harshest habitats on Earth: the deep, dark bottom of the ocean. Female anglerfish have rods protruding from their heads, and they create light at the tip of it to lure and catch their prey. Most anglerfish are less than 30 centimetres long, but they can swallow prey up to twice their own size!

B

BLUE WHALE

Habitat: Open ocean

Size: 20 to 30 metres long

Diet: Small crustaceans

The blue whale is the largest animal to ever live, with some fully mature whales growing to more than 30 metres long. Even though it is the biggest animal on Earth, its diet consists of very small animals called krill. Each day a blue whale can eat 5 tonnes of krill – that's the same weight as an elephant! Baby blue whales are huge too – they are about 7 m long when they are born.

B

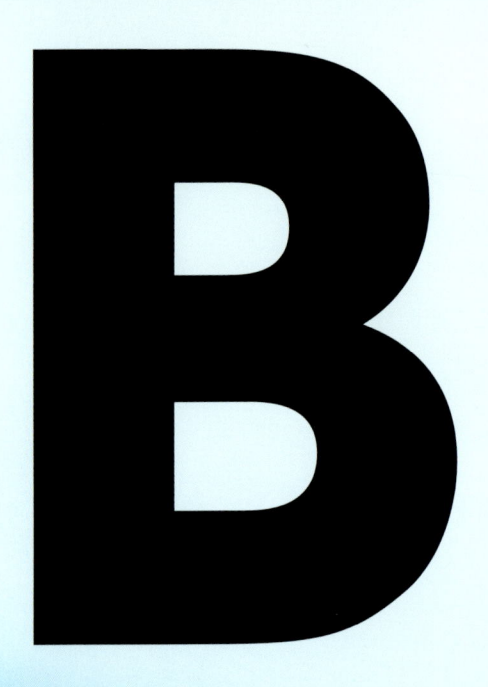

BULL SHARK

Habitat: Coastal waters and rivers

Size: Up to 3.4 metres long

Diet: Fish, crustaceans, birds, turtles and dolphins

Although bull sharks live in warm, shallow seas, they often swim up rivers too. These aggressive sharks are large and heavy with short snouts and about 50 sharp teeth. These fierce predators can often be found in parts of the ocean humans frequent and have been known to attack out of curiosity. Bull sharks are fast, agile hunters and will eat almost anything, including fish, dolphins and even other sharks.

BUTTERFLY FISH

Habitat: Warm shallow seas, especially coral reefs
Size: 13 to 30 centimetres long
Diet: Algae and invertebrates, especially coral polyps and anemones

With an amazing array of colours and stripes, butterfly fish are most commonly found in the warm seas surrounding coral reefs. These tricky fish have dark circles around their eyes, as well as eyelike markings on their flanks to confuse predators. Sometimes butterfly fish travel in small shoals, or groups, but usually they live alone until they mate for life.

C

CROWN OF THORNS STARFISH

Habitat: Warm shallow seas, especially coral reefs

Size: 25 to 35 centimetres wide

Diet: Coral polyps

The crown of thorns starfish lives in the Indian and Pacific Oceans and is one of the largest starfish in the world. With an appetite for coral, scientists consider this a species of concern because of how destructive it is – an adult crown of thorns starfish can eat over 9.3 square metres of coral in a year! Not only do these starfish threaten coral reefs, but the spines on their arms and bodies are also extremely poisonous to animals and humans.

CRUSTACEAN

Habitat: Various

Size: Various

Diet: Mostly algae and invertebrates

Crustaceans are invertebrate animals that belong to around 45,000 different species around the world. These creatures most commonly live in water and have eyes on stalks and a tough **exoskeleton**, or shell. The Japanese spider crab is one of the largest crustaceans on Earth and can weigh as much as 18 kilograms! The smallest are shrimps that weigh less than a pea.

C

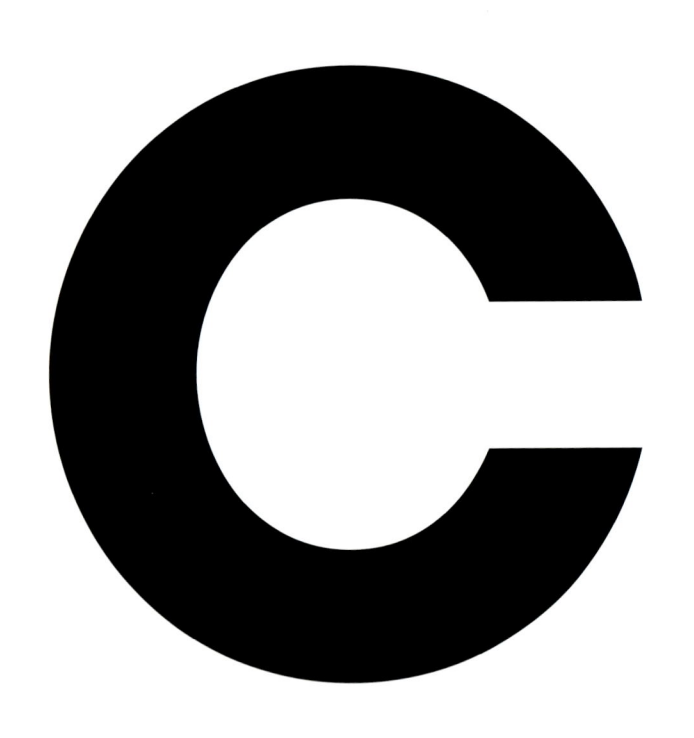

CORAL REEFS

Coral reefs are the most diverse ecosystems under the sea and are built by tiny animals called coral polyps. A coral reef may be home to billions of creatures and is one of the most important ocean habitats.

Coral Polyps

There are two kinds of coral polyps: stony and soft corals. Stony coral polyps create their skeletons by releasing calcium carbonate, which is a hard substance found in rocks. When those coral polyps die, new polyps will make their homes in the skeletons left behind. Over thousands of years, many colonies of stony corals create a reef.

Where Corals Grow

Most coral reefs grow near the coast in warm, shallow water that is clean. Coral polyps have green algae that live in their tissues. The green algae needs plenty of sunlight to make food for the coral polyps through **photosynthesis**.

Deep-sea corals grow in cold, dark water deep in the ocean. They do not have green algae in their tissues, so they have to catch their own food.

The Great Barrier Reef

The Great Barrier Reef off the coast of Australia is the world's largest reef. It is more than 2400 kilometres long, and it is home to 1500 species of fish, 4000 types of molluscs, and 14 species of sea snakes.

D

DIATOM

Habitat: To depths of around 200 metres
Size: Microscopic
Diet: Sunlight

Diatoms are microscopic algae vital to the survival of many sea creatures. Billions and billions of diatoms float in the ocean and use sunlight to make food through photosynthesis, just like land plants. There are over 16,000 species of diatoms that can be found on Earth, many of which are important sources of food for ocean animals.

DOG WHELK

Habitat: Rocky shores and estuaries

Size: Up to 6 centimetres long

Diet: Molluscs and crustaceans

A dog whelk is a type of sea snail that lives around rocky shores of the Atlantic Ocean. It is a member of the mollusc family, and it has a spiral-shaped shell. The dog whelks' favourite foods are mussels and barnacles, which they eat by piercing the shell, digesting the mussels and barnacles in their shells and then sucking out the resulting liquid.

D

DOLPHIN

Habitat: Open ocean and coastal waters

Size: 1.3 to 4 metres long

Diet: Fish and invertebrates

Some of the smartest and most sociable **mammals** in the oceans are dolphins. With a very distinct curved mouth and many cone-shaped teeth, dolphins often look like they are smiling! A dolphin's diet mostly consists of fish and squid, and they are able to communicate with each other using **echolocation**. These marine mammals live and hunt in groups called pods and usually have one calf, or baby dolphin, that will stay with its mother for up to six years.

D

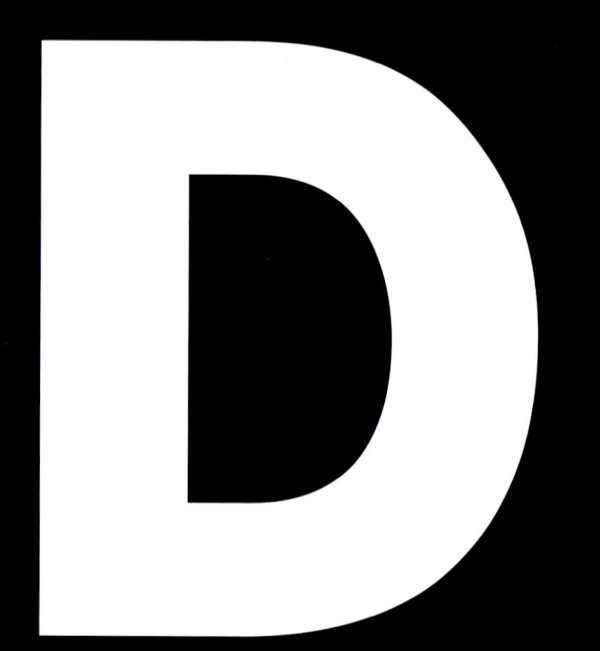

DEEP, DARK SEA

Very little sunlight can pass through sea water below a depth of around 200 metres. Here, the ocean turns dark and cold. Below a depth of around 1000 metres, there is no sunlight at all. This habitat is called the midnight zone.

Life in the Dark

Many deep-sea creatures are blind, but some animals that live deep in the ocean have very large eyes that can see in the dim light. There may not be any sunlight, but some deep sea animals can create light themselves!

Bio-light

Light that is made by animals is called bioluminescence. These animals have special chemicals in their bodies that can make light.

Deep-sea anglerfish have a bony piece of spine sticking out above their mouth that looks a bit like a fishing rod. At the end of the rod is bioluminescent flesh that lures small fish into swimming close enough for the anglerfish to swallow them up.

Deep-sea dragonfish create light at the tip of an antenna-like rod on their chin to find their prey and use their sharp teeth to catch them.

Hawaiian bobtail squid are nocturnal and have a light organ where bioluminescent bacteria live and create light in the squid's **mantle** to hide its shadow when it hunts at night.

E

ECHINODERM

Habitat: Seabed
Size: Up to 2 metres long
Diet: Various

Starfish, sea cucumbers and sea urchins are examples of echinoderms. A large group of invertebrate marine animals, most echinoderms have hard, spiny skin. There are over 6500 species of echinoderms, and they are found in every level of the ocean. Echinoderms have been in existence for generations and scientists have identified more than 13,000 fossil species of echinoderms!

EEL

Habitat: Open oceans, coasts and rivers

Size: Up to 2.7 metres long

Diet: Fish and invertebrates

Eels are long, snakelike bony fishes with flexible bodies. For most of their lives, eels swim alone and either live in the cracks and crevices of rocks or dig holes by burrowing deep into the sand with their pointy tails. There are over 800 different species of eels, including morays, congers and deep-sea eels.

E

EMPEROR PENGUIN

Habitat: Cold seas and coasts

Size: 1.1 metre tall

Diet: Fish and invertebrates

On the ice-cold continent of Antarctica, emperor penguins spend their lives surviving the harsh weather conditions. Like other penguins, they hunt fish and squid in the cold seas. Penguins are flightless birds, so they use their wings like flippers to swim. Emperor penguins breed in the winter, and after the females lay one egg each, the males stand in the freezing cold for 65 days while keeping the eggs safe and warm!

F

FANGTOOTH FISH

Habitat: Deep ocean
Size: 18 centimetres long
Diet: Fish and crustaceans

Despite it being one of the most inhospitable environments on Earth, many strange animals live in the deep, dark oceans, including the fangtooth fish. These fish are small, but they have very long, sharp teeth that are perfect for catching slippery squid. Scientists have found the fangtooth fish as deep as 5 kilometres below the surface, making it one of the deepest-dwelling fish in the ocean.

FEATHER STAR

Habitat: Seabed

Size: Up to 40 centimetres wide

Diet: Plankton

Feather stars are marine invertebrates with five arms. When they first grow, feather stars are attached to a long stalk, but as they get bigger, they break off from the stalk and use their grasping legs to attach themselves to sponges or coral. These feathery echinoderms feed on floating microorganisms that they trap using their sticky arm grooves.

FLYING FISH

Habitat: Surface waters

Size: Up to 45 centimetres long

Diet: Mostly plankton

In warm ocean waters around the world, flying fish can be seen gliding through the air. In order to leap out of the water, these agile fish have to reach underwater speeds of about 60 kilometres per hour! Flying fish are so skilful they can leap about a metre high and glide up to 180 metres before returning to the water.

F

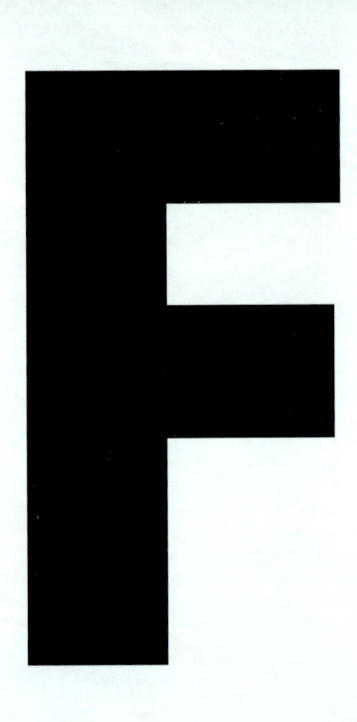

FISH

Most fish have long, tube-shaped bodies, fins and scaly skin. They use gills to breathe underwater, and they have strong muscles in their tails for swimming.

Sharks and Rays

Sharks and rays belong to a group of fish that have skeletons made of **cartilage** instead of bone. Rays are flat fish that spend most of their lives on the seafloor, while sharks are large, fast-swimming predators. There are more than 850 species of fish with cartilaginous skeletons.

Bony Fish

Most fish are bony fish, with skeletons made of hard bone. There are at least 28,000 species of bony fish and many of them have protective scales covering their bodies.

Shape and Size

Long, slender fish are often fast swimmers. Other fish, such as the frogfish, use leglike fins to crawl on the seafloor. Scientists often use size and shape to identify different species of fish.

G

GARIBALDI

Habitat: Warm, shallow water
Size: 30 centimetres long
Diet: Invertebrates

These colourful fish live in the shallow waters of the Pacific Ocean, often along rocky shores with plenty of seaweed. Adult garibaldi are bright orange, making them very recognizable. Before mating, male garibaldi meticulously construct circular nests to attract females. Once the females lay their eggs, the males fend off any predators by making a loud thumping noise.

GIANT CLAM

Habitat: Warm, shallow water
Size: Up to 1.5 metres wide
Diet: Plankton and food made by the clam's algae

Giant clams are the largest molluscs in the world, growing more than 1.2 metres wide and weighing over 225 kilograms! Giant clams grow in warm, sunny ocean waters and once they attach themselves to a reef, that becomes their permanent home. These clams grow to be giants thanks to the green algae that live in their tissues and create food through photosynthesis.

GIANT TUBE WORM

Habitat: Seabed
Size: Up to 3 metres tall
Diet: Food made by bacteria

In the cold, dark depths of the ocean, giant tube worms have adapted to their harsh environment by making their homes on the edge of hydrothermal vents. These mouthless, gutless tube worms are one of the fastest growing animals on Earth. They have a **symbiotic** relationship with bacteria that can convert the chemicals released from the vents into food for the tube worms, allowing them to thrive in an otherwise inhospitable environment.

H

HAMMERHEAD SHARK

Habitat: Warm, coastal waters

Size: 1 to 6 metres long

Diet: Fish and invertebrates

One of the most interesting shark species in the oceans is the hammerhead. Aptly named, these sharks have hammer-shaped heads that can detect and pin down their favourite food: stingrays. There are nine species of hammerheads, the largest of which is the 6-metre-long great hammerhead shark. Some sharks lay eggs, but these unusual-looking sharks give birth to live babies, which are called pups.

HUMPBACK WHALE

Habitat: Open ocean and coastal waters

Size: Up to 17 metres long

Diet: Krill and small fish

These marine giants are found in every ocean on Earth. Humpback whales feed in cool oceans during the summer, and in the winter they migrate to warmer seas to give birth to their young. Like most whales, humpbacks feast on large amounts of krill and other small animals. Like dolphins, humpback whales communicate with each other through 'songs' that can travel great distances in the ocean.

I

IRUKANDJI JELLYFISH

Habitat: Warm, coastal waters
Size: Less than 2.5 centimetres long
Diet: Small invertebrates, crustaceans and fish

Despite its extremely small size, the Irukandji jellyfish has the undeserved reputation of being one of the deadliest creatures in coastal reef waters around the world. Because they are so small and translucent, they are very hard to spot in the water. Their stings can be extremely painful.

ISOPOD

Habitat: Seabed

Size: Up to 30 centimetres long

Diet: Dead animals, plants and algae

These widely occurring species can be found in the oceans, fresh water and on land. There are over 10,000 species of isopods, which come in many shapes and sizes. Giant isopods are crustaceans that can grow as large as a cat and live in the cold, dark depths of the oceans. They eat anything they can find on the seabed, from sea slugs and worms to the rotting bodies of dead fish.

INVERTEBRATES

Invertebrates are animals that do not have backbones, such as jellyfish and anemones. Most ocean invertebrates are small or even microscopic, but some of them can grow to be very big – much bigger than invertebrates on land. There have been invertebrates in the oceans for more than 580 million years!

Plankton

The tiny invertebrate animals, algae and plants that drift in the ocean are called plankton. Many of them are so small they can only be seen with a microscope! Plankton mostly float near the surface of the water, and many larger animals, and even some whales, eat them.

Types of Ocean Invertebrates:

- Cnidarians
- Crustaceans
- Echinoderms
- Molluscs
- Sponges
- Marine worms

Staying Strong

Invertebrates do not have bones, but many of them grow shells to protect their soft bodies. Some **cnidarians** build rocky cups to sit in, while others defend themselves with stingers instead.

Sponges

Sponges are very simple invertebrates that live on the seafloor or in coral reefs. They use tiny tentacles to catch food that drifts past them in the water.

J

JACKASS PENGUIN

Habitat: Coasts and islands
Size: 45 centimetres tall
Diet: Fish, squid and crustaceans

Only found on the rocky shores of southern Africa, the jackass penguin is more commonly referred to as the African penguin. They use their beaks and feet to dig burrows on the beach, where they lay two eggs at a time. These penguins mate for life, so while one is hunting fish, the other will stay behind and guard their nest. Because the fish population is decreasing off the coast of southern Africa, jackass penguins are considered an endangered species.

JAPANESE SPIDER CRAB

Habitat: Seabed

Size: Leg span of 3 metres

Diet: Dead animals, plants and algae

With the title of largest crab in the ocean, Japanese spider crabs weigh around 18 kilograms. These giant crabs live primarily in shallow water around Japan. Their legs are long and weak, so they are prone to lose at least one leg over the course of their impressive 100-year lifespan!

J

JELLYFISH

Habitat: Open ocean and coastal waters
Size: Body is 2.5 centimetres to 2 metres wide
Diet: Plankton, invertebrates and fish

Despite their name, jellyfish are not actually fish. They belong to a group of soft-bodied animals called cnidarians. Adult jellyfish have bell-shaped bodies with many long, stinging tentacles that they use to catch and kill their prey. Although jellyfish can swim, they mostly drift along on ocean currents with their tentacles trailing behind them.

49

K

KELP

Habitat: Seabed in sunlit waters

Size: Up to 30 metres long

Kelp is a type of brown algae that can grow into huge undersea forests. A single strand of kelp can grow up to 46 centimetres in just one day and can grow to be 30 metres long! Kelp forests make great homes for many ocean animals, including fish, sea urchins and sea otters, because they provide plenty of food and shelter.

KILLER WHALE

Habitat: Open ocean and coastal waters

Size: Up to 9 metres long

Diet: Squid, fish, birds and marine mammals

Also known as orcas, killer whales are large black-and-white dolphins. The largest dolphins in the ocean, orcas are very intelligent and travel in large family groups, or pods, that hunt together. They are often found in cold, coastal waters, and each pod works as a team to hunt fish and large marine mammals, such as seals and whale calves.

K

KITTIWAKE

Habitat: Coastal cliffs

Size: 38 to 40 centimetres long

Diet: Fish, shrimps and worms

Kittiwakes belong to a group of seabirds called gulls. They build their nests from seaweed and mud on steep cliff edges along the Atlantic coast, but they spend most of the year at sea. Kittiwakes are very noisy birds, and they catch fish by diving into the water while in flight. If there is not enough fish to eat, kittiwakes will also eat molluscs, small squid or insects.

KRILL

Habitat: Open ocean and coastal waters

Size: Up to 7.5 centimetres long

Diet: Plankton (plants and algae)

Some of the ocean's most important creatures are the smallest. Krill are shrimplike crustaceans that serve as the main food source of hundreds of different animals, such as whales, birds and fish. This tiny species usually grows no bigger than a finger, but there are billions of them in the seas. Many ecosystems in and around the oceans depend on krill.

L

LEAFY SEA DRAGON

Habitat: Shallow water with kelp or sea grass
Size: 30 centimetres long
Diet: Shrimps and plankton

These are one of the most camouflaged creatures on Earth. Leafy sea dragons live in shallow waters around Australia, where they blend almost perfectly into the seaweed. Closely related to seahorses, female sea dragons also lay eggs in a special pouch on the male's tail. Once the eggs have been transferred, the male takes care of the eggs until they are ready to hatch.

LEATHERBACK SEA TURTLE

Habitat: Open ocean and coastal waters

Size: 1.4 to 2.1 metres long

Diet: Jellyfish

There are seven species of sea turtles, of which the leatherback is the largest, growing up to 2.1 metres long and weighing over 910 kilograms! These massive turtles feed mostly on invertebrates such as jellyfish, so they have spines in their throats to keep their slippery prey from escaping. Like other sea turtles, these reptiles spend most of their lives at sea, but the females travel to sandy beaches to lay their eggs.

L

LIONFISH

Habitat: Warm, coastal waters
Size: Up to 38 centimetres long
Diet: Fish and crustaceans

Because lionfish are such slow swimmers, they rely on their bold stripes and sharp, venomous spines to protect them from predators. Lionfish are native to the South Pacific and Indian Oceans, but can also be found in the Atlantic, where they are considered an invasive species. Because they are not native to the Atlantic Ocean, they are one of the top predators and are destroying many Atlantic ecosystems.

LOBSTER

Habitat: Seabed

Size: Up to 60 centimetres long

Diet: Fish and invertebrates

Lobsters are long-bodied, bottom-dwelling crustaceans. The largest ones can grow to be more than 60 centimetres long and have five pairs of legs. The first pair of legs are huge claws that can be used as pincers to catch and crush prey. One of the most common lobsters is the American lobster, which is one of the most heavily harvested creatures in the ocean.

M

MANGROVE

Habitat: Warm coasts

Size: 1 to 65 metres tall

A mangrove is a tree that lives in seawater in hot environments. They have long, stringy roots that trap mud and help to slow the flow of water at the coast. Many animals and plants, from crabs and birds to howler monkeys, find a home in mangroves.

MOLLUSC

Habitat: Various

Size: Up to 16.8 metres long

Diet: Various

There are about 80,000 species of molluscs, and most of them live in the world's oceans. Most species are invertebrates with soft bodies that are sometimes partially or wholly enclosed in a shell. Squid, octopus and sea slugs are examples of molluscs. Shellfish are also molluscs that have one or two shells to protect themselves.

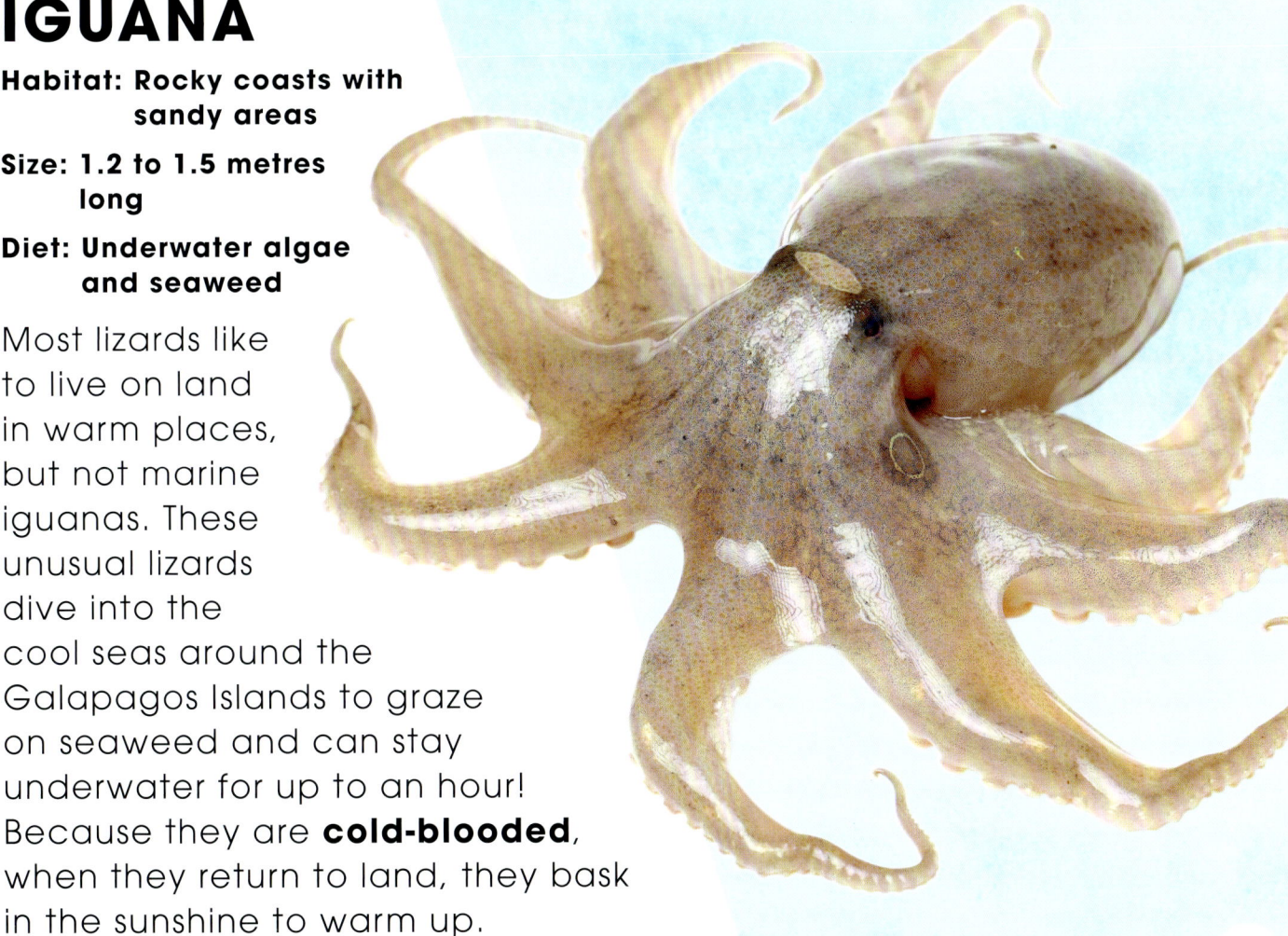

MARINE IGUANA

Habitat: Rocky coasts with sandy areas

Size: 1.2 to 1.5 metres long

Diet: Underwater algae and seaweed

Most lizards like to live on land in warm places, but not marine iguanas. These unusual lizards dive into the cool seas around the Galapagos Islands to graze on seaweed and can stay underwater for up to an hour! Because they are **cold-blooded**, when they return to land, they bask in the sunshine to warm up.

MAMMALS

Most mammals live on land, but there are some mammals that make their homes in the ocean. Unlike fish, ocean mammals cannot breathe underwater, so they have to breach the surface to breathe air. Because mammals are **warm-blooded**, some ocean mammals have thick fur to keep them warm, while others have thick layers of blubber.

There are three main groups of ocean mammals.

Whales

Whales, dolphins and porpoises spend their whole lives in water. They come to the surface to breathe, using blowholes on the tops of their heads. They give birth underwater and hunt ocean animals to eat.

Seals

Seals, sea lions and walruses are strong swimmers that hunt fish and other sea creatures. They return to land to rest and give birth to their young, which are called pups.

Dugongs and Manatees

Dugongs and manatees can stay underwater for up to 20 minutes at a time, and feed on plants. These ocean mammals are related to elephants, even though they don't look anything like them!

N

NARWHAL

Habitat: Cold ocean water
Size: Up to 4.7 metres long
Diet: Fish, squid and crustaceans

Narwhals are sometimes called the unicorns of the sea. They are a kind of whale that live in the Arctic Ocean. Males have long, spiralled tusks growing from their snouts. Scientists believe that a narwhal's tusk, which is actually an enlarged tooth, may play a big part in attracting a mate. Narwhals, like dolphins and other whales, live in groups and feed on fish, shrimps and squid.

NAUTILUS

Habitat: Warm oceans, near the seabed

Size: Up to 20 centimetres wide

Diet: Dead animals, shrimps and crabs

The nautilus is a mollusc that has a shell and is even older than the dinosaurs! The nautilus's shell is divided into chambers, with the body residing in the largest chamber. The other chambers hold water to help the nautilus to float. When water flows into the living chamber, the nautilus is able to shoot the water out and swim. They are often harvested for their pretty shells, which is why scientists consider them a species vulnerable to overfishing.

O

OCEAN SUNFISH

Habitat: Warm waters in the open ocean

Size: Up to 3 metres long

Diet: Jellyfish, molluscs, crustaceans and plankton

Ocean sunfish, or mola, are giant bony fish that swim in the open ocean. These fish look like floating blobs because their back fin never grows, giving them a slightly circular shape. Often found in tropical oceans, they tend to lie on their sides near the surface of the water, basking in the sun and eating jellyfish and other small, floating animals.

OCTOPUS

Habitat: Coral reefs or the ocean floor

Size: Up to 9 metres long

Diet: Various

Octopuses are molluscs that have large heads, eight arms and no shells. They are intelligent animals that can solve problems, change colour, and even change shape. There are about 300 different species of octopus. Octopuses are extremely fast swimmers, making it easier for them to escape predators. If an octopus gets caught, it can lose an arm to the predator and then regrow it later!

O

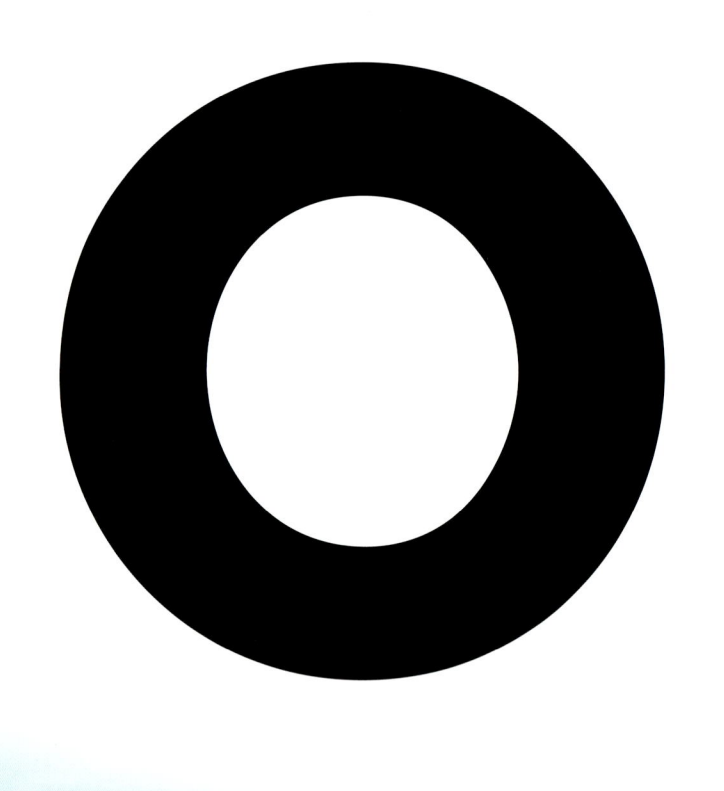

OTTER

Habitat: Kelp forests
Size: 1 to 1.5 metres long
Diet: Fish and invertebrates

One of the cutest marine mammals, sea otters live in kelp forests in the Pacific Ocean, where they feed on sea urchins, shellfish and crustaceans. They live in close family groups and baby sea otters sleep on their mother's belly as she floats on her back. Otters are famous for holding hands as they float on the surface of the water!

OYSTERCATCHER

Habitat: Coasts, lagoons and salt marshes

Size: Up to 45 centimetres long

Diet: Invertebrates, especially molluscs

Oystercatchers are long-legged birds with orange beaks that wade through the soft mud along the coast. Their brightly coloured beaks are long, strong and perfect for digging shellfish out of the mud and cracking them open. Oystercatchers make their nests on the ground and lay their eggs in the sand!

O

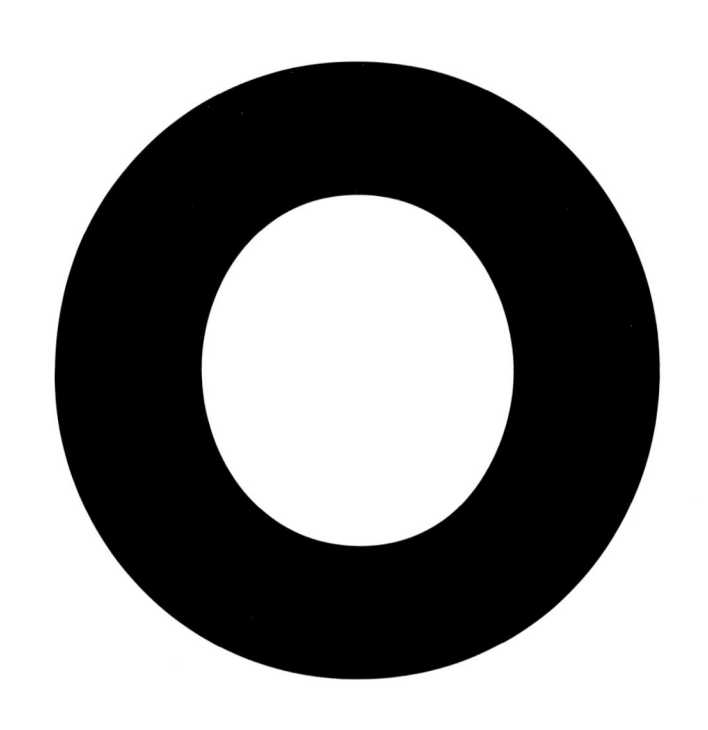

OPEN OCEAN

The open ocean is huge and includes all of the world's oceans except for coastal waters and the seafloor. The animals that live in the open ocean may never come to land or visit the seafloor.

Huge Habitat

The open ocean is the largest habitat on Earth. Animals that live here move around by swimming or drifting in the water. Whales, fish and turtles swim, while jellyfish and plankton drift and are carried by ocean currents.

Up and Down

The open ocean can be a dangerous place to live because there are not many places to hide. Many small ocean animals move down to the deeper levels of the ocean and spend the daytime safely hiding in the dark. At night, they swim up to the surface of the sea to feed on plankton.

Schools of Fish

A group of fish is called a school. Large schools of fast fish swim through the open ocean. Many of them have silvery scales that reflect sunlight, causing them to shimmer as they dart through the water. This makes it difficult for predators to see individuals clearly.

P

PEACOCK MANTIS SHRIMP

Habitat: Shallow-water seabed
Size: 2.5 to 18 centimetres long
Diet: Crustaceans, molluscs and fish

A peacock mantis shrimp may look small, but it has a powerful punch! This colourful crustacean has great eyesight, and when it sees danger, or something good to eat, it acts fast. It will use its claws to hit its prey with great speed and strength. The punch is strong enough to crush a crab or even smash through glass!

POLAR BEAR

Habitat: Sea ice and cold coastal waters

Size: 1.8 to 2.4 metres long

Diet: Seals, walruses, seabirds, fish and whales

Polar bears are the world's only marine bears. They are huge, powerful mammals that live on the sea ice around the Arctic, where they hunt seals. Because their home is so cold, polar bears have thick fur and layers of fat that help to keep them warm. They are also very strong swimmers, helped by their slightly webbed toes!

PORTUGUESE MAN O' WAR

Habitat: Surface of the ocean

Size: 'Body' length of 30 centimetres

Diet: Fish, crustaceans and plankton

A Portuguese man o' war looks like a floating jellyfish, but it is actually a colony of tiny animals called polyps. They have many long, stinging tentacles that hang down from a balloon-shaped 'body' that floats on the water. As fish swim past, they are trapped by the tentacles and stung to death. The man o' war's sting is not nearly as deadly for humans, but it is very painful, and they can still sting even when they're dead!

P

PUFFER FISH

Habitat: Warm, coastal waters

Size: Up to 1 metre long

Diet: Invertebrates and algae

Because they are one of the more clumsy fish in the sea, puffer fish swallow water (or air!) until their entire body swells and spikes on their skin stand up. Not only do the fish look big and scary when this happens, but it also makes it very hard for predators to eat them. Puffer fish are also extremely poisonous – there is enough poison in one puffer fish to kill 30 humans!

73

P

PLANTS AND ALGAE

Plants are living things that use sunlight, air and water to make their food. The process of using sunlight to turn carbon dioxide and water into food is called photosynthesis. Most plants have roots that grow into the soil and stems and leaves that grow up towards the light.

Marine Plants

Marine plants grow in shallow water along the coasts, where there is enough sunshine for photosynthesis. Sea grasses and mangrove trees are examples of marine plants. Sea grasses, such as eelgrass, grow underwater on sandy and rocky seafloors. Mangrove trees grow along the coast.

Algae

Algae are also living things that use sunlight for photosynthesis. They do not have roots or stems, and they can be green, red or brown. Most algae are tiny and float near the surface of the sea. Seaweed is a larger form of algae.

Food for All

Plants and algae are very important sources of food for ocean animals. Plants also help the planet by taking carbon dioxide, a gas that is making the Earth get warmer, and turning it into oxygen, a gas that we need to breathe.

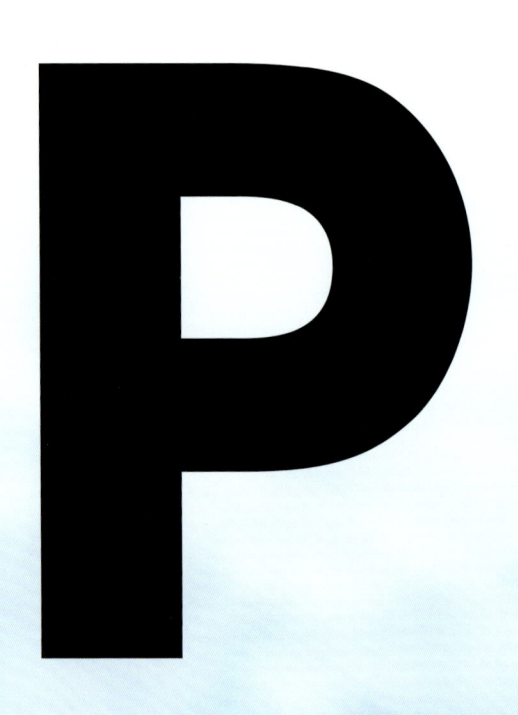

POLAR OCEANS

The Arctic Ocean and the Southern Ocean are the world's coldest oceans. They are covered in huge sheets of ice for most of the year, but they are an important wildlife habitat.

The Arctic Ocean

The Arctic Ocean is the smallest of the Earth's five oceans. During the winter, the ocean around the North Pole is covered in a thick layer of ice. During the short summer, half of that ice melts.

The Southern Ocean

The Southern Ocean surrounds the Antarctic, which is a huge area of land that covers the South Pole. There are massive ice sheets that stretch from the land far out into the sea. These sheets of ice can be very thick.

Q

QUEEN ANGELFISH

Habitat: Coral reefs

Size: Up to 46 centimetres long

Diet: Sponges, algae, coral and jellyfish

These beautiful fish are usually the most colourful fish in any reef. Queen angelfish are foragers that mostly eat sponges, algae and occasionally soft corals. They are usually seen swimming along in the warm waters of the Caribbean Sea and Atlantic Ocean but they are quick to find a hiding place when disturbed. Even with their bright colours, queen angelfish can hide in a colourful reef.

QUEEN SCALLOP

Habitat: Seabed in coastal waters

Size: Up to 9 centimetres wide

Diet: Plankton

The queen scallop is a mollusc that lives in the cool waters of the Atlantic Ocean. It is a bivalve, which means it has two shells that open and close at a hinge. When the scallop is young, fine threads grow from the hinge and attach to the seabed. When the scallop is older, it loses those threads and can swim by quickly opening and closing its shells to propel itself through the water!

R

80

RAY

Habitat: Open ocean, seabed and coastal waters

Size: Up to 8 metres wide

Diet: Fish, invertebrates and plankton

Rays are flat fish that are closely related to sharks. There are over 600 different species of rays, the largest of which is the manta ray. Rays spend most of their time on the seafloor, camouflaged against the sandy bottom. While most rays prefer to bury themselves in sand, they are all able to swim – some by moving their bodies in a wave pattern, and others by flapping their fins like wings.

R

REMORA FISH

Habitat: Warm, open ocean
Size: Up to 46 centimetres long
Diet: Plankton, fish and food scraps

Remoras are also known as suckerfish. They have a large disc on their heads that they use to stick to other, bigger fish, especially sharks. Remoras use this trick to get carried around the ocean without having to spend any energy on swimming. Found in warm water, remoras are 'cleaner' fish, so they eat scraps and parasites found on their hosts!

ROBBER CRAB

Habitat: Warm, coastal areas

Size: Leg span of up to 1 metre

Diet: Dead animals, fruit and coconuts

Also known as the coconut crab, robber crabs spend much of their lives on land, but lay their eggs in water. This giant crustacean is a scavenger that feeds mostly on fallen fruit or the shells of other crabs. They have been known to crack open coconuts with their strong pincers, hence their nickname!

R

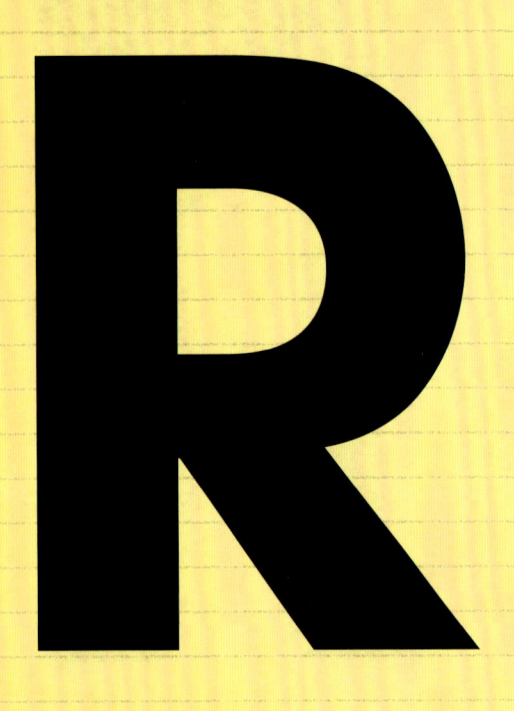

REPTILES

Reptiles are cold-blooded vertebrates that are covered in scales. Most of them lay eggs on land.

There are four main types of reptiles that can live in the ocean:

- Turtles
- Lizards
- Snakes
- Crocodiles

Turtles

There are seven species of marine turtles. They have bony shells that protect their bodies, and they have flippers for swimming. Female marine turtles lay their eggs on land.

Lizards

Lizards are reptiles with four legs and a long tail. Almost all lizards live on land, but a few species, such as the marine iguana and some monitor lizards, find food in the ocean.

Snakes

Sea snakes have long, slender bodies and no legs, just like land snakes. Instead of slithering on land, they swim near the surface of the sea. Most sea snakes live in warm oceans.

Crocodiles

The crocodile family includes crocodiles, alligators and caimans, most of which live in fresh water or in swampy water near the seashore. Saltwater crocodiles are strong swimmers that often hunt fish in the open ocean.

S

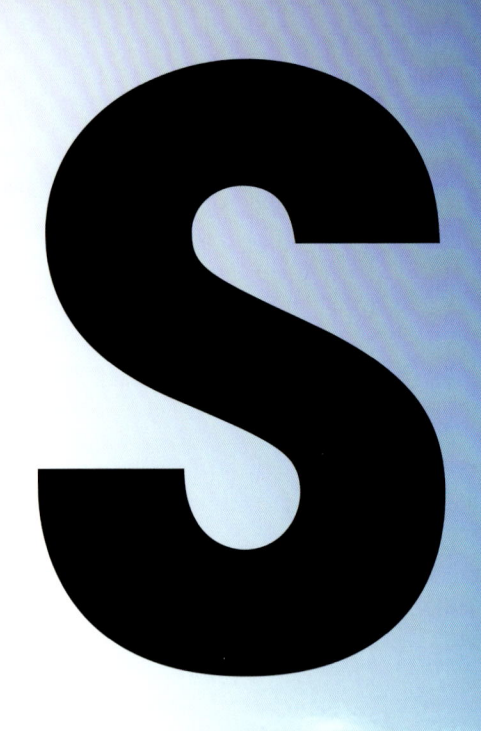

SEAHORSE

Habitat: Sheltered coastal waters
Size: 1 to 33 centimetres long
Diet: Crustaceans, mostly shrimps

Seahorses are small fish with curly tails that they use to hold on to seaweed. They reproduce in a special way, with the female laying dozens of eggs in a male's brood pouch. The male then takes care of the eggs until they hatch. Unlike most fish, seahorses do not have scales. Instead, their skin is stretched over strong, bony plates that work like a suit of armour!

SEA SLUG

Habitat: Mostly on or near the seabed

Size: Up to 1 metre long

Diet: Various

Part of the mollusc family, sea slugs are shell-less bottom-dwellers. While most sea slugs crawl along the seabed, some are able to swim or float. Many sea slugs are poisonous, and they use their bright colours to stop predators from eating them!

S SHARK

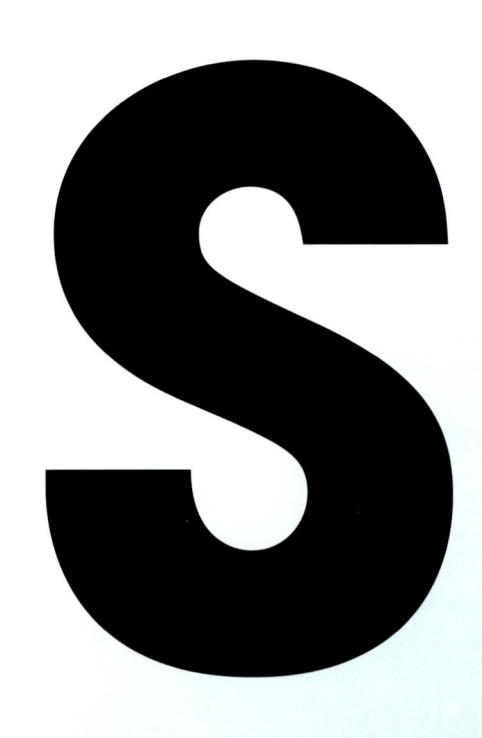

Habitat: Seabed, open ocean and coastal areas

Size: Up to 18.8 metres

Diet: Fish, invertebrates, mammals, seabirds and plankton

Sharks have swum in the oceans for at least 400 million years. They have been able to adapt to suit a changing world and today there are about 500 species of shark. A shark's skeleton is made of cartilage, a tough material that is more flexible than bone. Most sharks are fierce predators with razor-sharp serrated teeth they use to eat ocean animals, such as seals. A shark's mouth is lined with rows of teeth that routinely fall out and grow back!

89

S

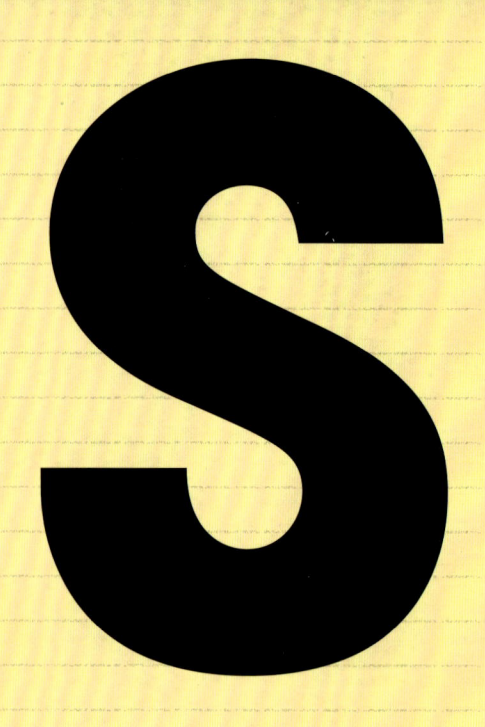

SEABIRDS

There are hundreds of seabird species that can be found in different habitats around the world. Not only do many birds rely on the ocean for food, but birds are also very important to the ocean's many ecosystems.

Waders

Many birds, such as sandpipers and snipes, have long legs and wide, webbed feet that are great for wading in shallow water at the coast. They use their long, slender beaks to find food buried in the mud or to grab small fish.

Divers

Some birds, including loons and gannets, soar above the ocean and search for signs of life in the water below. They dive headfirst into the water to grab fish and squid. Some diving birds can stay underwater for several minutes, searching for food or chasing fish.

Penguins

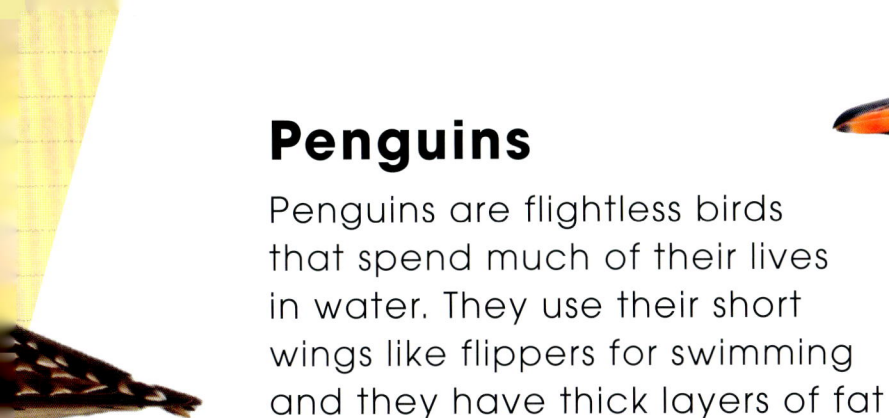

Penguins are flightless birds that spend much of their lives in water. They use their short wings like flippers for swimming and they have thick layers of fat beneath their feathers to keep them warm in cold seas.

Nesting

Seabirds often fly long distances before nesting on the sides of steep cliffs near the ocean. One such bird is the common murre, which makes its nest on coastal cliffs in Oregon, United States.

S

SOS – SAVE OUR SEAS

The oceans and their wildlife are in danger due to humans overfishing and polluting the planet.

Overfishing

People hunt fish and other marine animals to ea If too many fish are taken from the sea, they ma go **extinct**, causing other animals that rely on them for food to starve.

Pollution

Pollution is something that harms the natural world. Plastic pollution is damaging many animals and their habitats in the oceans. For example, scientists have found that 52 per cent of the world's sea turtles have eaten plastic bags because they look like jellyfish. Many sea turtles and other marine animals die after eating just one piece of plastic. Because plastic is not biodegradable, the plastic and other rubbish in the ocean has formed the Great Pacific Garbage Patch located off the eastern coast of Japan and the western coast of the United States.

Global Warming

Air pollution comes from burning fuels such as oil, coal or gas, which releases carbon dioxide into the air. Carbon dioxide traps the Sun's heat in the Earth's atmosphere, making the world warmer.

When the ocean temperature increases, the ice in the Arctic and Southern Oceans melts, and sea levels rise around the world. Rising sea levels can cause destructive erosion along coastlines, flooding and lost habitats for animals and plants.

Acidic Seas

Air pollution mixes with ocean water and makes it more acidic. This damages ocean wildlife, especially shellfish and corals. The more acidic the ocean gets, the faster coral reefs dissolve, which slows the growth of one of the ocean's most important habitats, threatening the survival of many species.

Conservation

Protecting wildlife and their habitats is called **conservation**. Some parts of the ocean have been turned into conservation areas, where fishing is not allowed and people work to keep those habitats free from pollution.

T

TERN

Habitat: Coasts and wetlands
Size: Up to 53 centimetres long
Diet: Fish, crustaceans and insects

With over 40 different species, terns are graceful water birds. Many terns migrate long distances, such as the Arctic tern, which flies across the oceans so it can spend all year enjoying summertime. This great migration covers nearly 70,000 kilometres and is the longest of any bird!

TIGER COWRIE

Habitat: Seabed in tropical waters
Size: Up to 15 centimetres long
Diet: Invertebrates and algae

Tiger cowries are molluscs with smooth, patterned shells covered with a thin film of skin. Also known as sea snails, they feed on coral, algae and sponges. Tiger cowries are commonly found in the warm, shallow waters of the Indian and Pacific Oceans. This species of sea snail is nocturnal – they are usually hiding from their predators (fish and octopus) during the day.

TIDES

Tides are the rise and fall of sea levels around the world. There are high tides and low tides each day. Low tide is when the sea is at its lowest level because the tide is out. When the tide comes in, at high tide, the whole beach can be covered by water.

Rock Pools

Rock pools, or tidal pools, are unique ecosystems found between the high and low tides on the coast. During low tide, water remains in bowl-like holes in rocks, which creates mini habitats for fish, crabs, shellfish, sea anemones and other ocean animals.

Plants and Algae

The water at the coast is shallow. This means sunlight can reach the seafloor, so many plants and algae grow well in rock pools. The plants and algae that grow there are an important source of food for the ocean animals that call rock pools their home.

Shelter

Rock pools provide safe homes for many ocean animals. Predators searching along the coast for their meals may have a hard time finding prey hiding among the seaweed and rocks.

UPSIDE-DOWN JELLYFISH

Habitat: Warm, coastal waters

Size: Up to 30 centimetres wide

Diet: Fish and food made by algae

Most jellyfish swim with their tentacles hanging down, but the upside-down jellyfish prefers to let its tentacles float above its bell-shaped body. This is because there are tiny green algae that live in the jellyfish's tentacles and photosynthesize. By giving the green algae enough sunlight, the upside-down jellyfish is also feeding itself!

URCHIN

Habitat: Seabed

Size: Shell up to 18 centimetres wide

Diet: Algae, plants and dead animals

Sea urchins are prickly echinoderms, some of which have venomous spines for protection. They have round bodies and tiny tube 'feet' that they use to slowly move along the seabed or rocky shore. Their mouths are on their underside, so as they move they graze for algae, barnacles and other food. When reproducing, a female urchin can release over a million eggs at a time!

V

VAMPIRE SQUID

Habitat: Deep ocean

Size: Up to 28 centimetres long

Diet: Dead remains of plants, algae and animals

The vampire squid is found in the deep, dark ocean, where it drifts as it feeds on bits of marine snow – tiny bits of dead animals and poo that sink into the deep ocean. As a defence mechanism, the unique vampire squid can squirt a cloud of sticky bioluminescent mucus towards would-be predators.

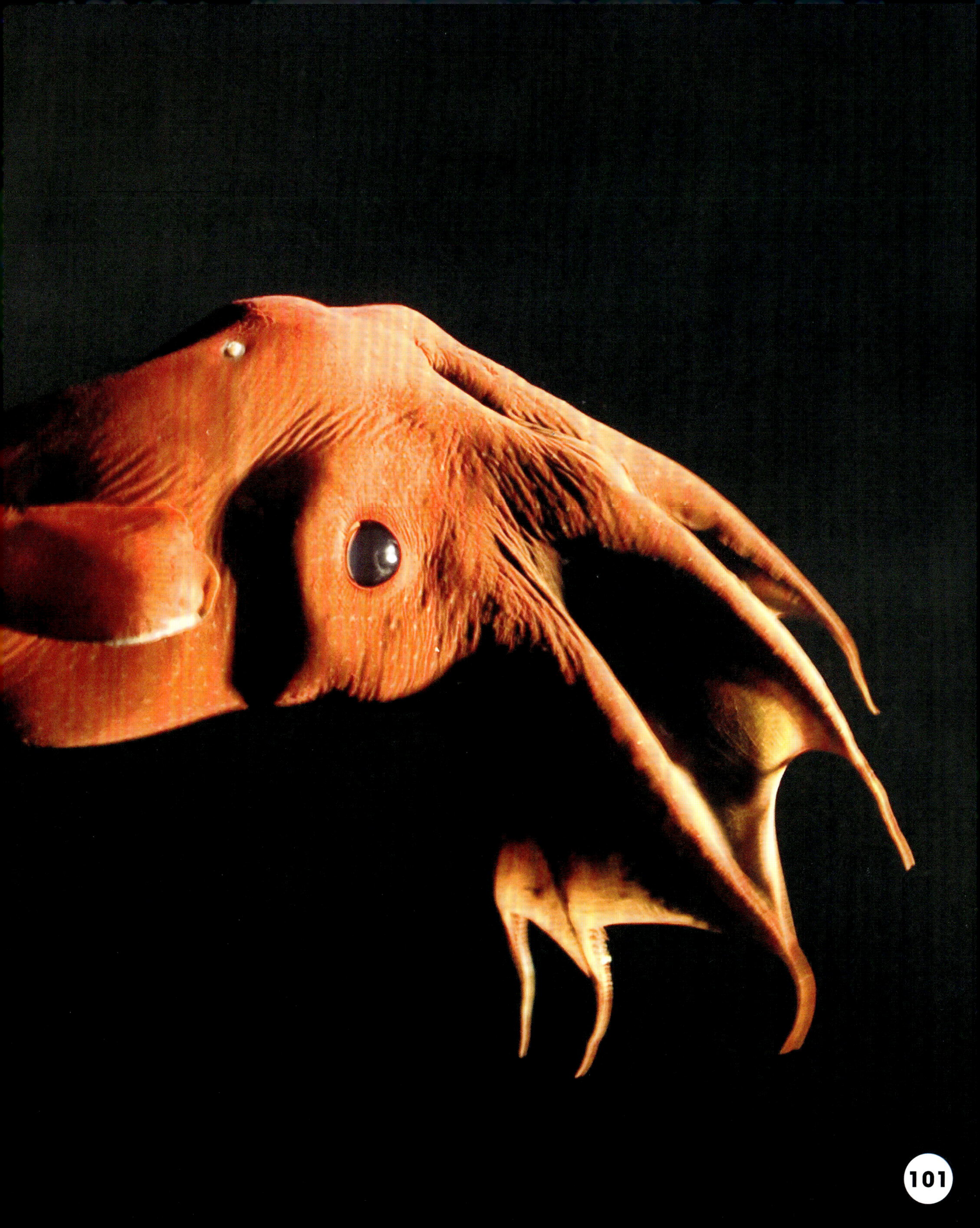

V

VAQUITA

Habitat: Warm, coastal waters
Size: Up to 1.5 metres long
Diet: Fish, squid and crustaceans

One of the world's rarest and most endangered animals is a small porpoise called the vaquita. It is a member of the whale family and lives in warm seas near Mexico, where it hunts fish. There are fewer than 20 adult vaquitas left in the whole world, which makes it a critically endangered species that will likely be extinct soon.

VENUS COMB

Habitat: Sandy seabed in warm, coastal waters

Size: Up to 15 centimetres long

Diet: Molluscs

Venus combs are molluscs that have many long spines on their shells. The spines protect the mollusc from being eaten and allow the animal to rest on the shore without being tossed around by the waves. Venus comb shells are most commonly found in the Indian and Pacific Oceans.

W

WALRUS

Habitat: Cold, coastal areas
Size: Up to 3.5 metres long
Diet: Shellfish

These moustachioed marine mammals live in the Atlantic and Pacific Oceans. They have flippers for swimming and two long tusks that can grow to be 1 metre long. They can live to be around 40 years old and can weigh over 1350 kilograms! A walrus's moustache isn't just for looks – they use their sensitive whiskers to find shellfish to eat on the dark ocean floor!

WATER MONITOR

Habitat: Warm, coastal areas

Size: Up to 2.7 metres long

Diet: Fish, crustaceans, birds, turtles, young crocodiles and dead animals

Most water monitors make their homes in rivers and lakes, but these lizards can also survive in salty water. They are strong swimmers, swishing their long tails from side to side. Water monitors are not picky eaters and will hunt almost anything they can find. They lay their eggs in burrows along the coast.

W

WHALE SHARK

Habitat: Warm oceans

Size: Up to 18.8 metres long

Diet: Small fish and plankton

The largest fish in the world is the whale shark. Even though it is massive, its favourite food is plankton. Whale sharks are filter feeders. They open their jaws wide and gulp mouthfuls of water. Their gills work like sieves to filter out the plankton, which is swallowed, and the water is passed out through the gills. This way, they waste very little energy actively hunting for food. Instead, they just let their gills do the work for them!

WORM

Habitat: In or near the seabed

Size: Up to 50 metres long

Diet: Various

Like most living things found in the ocean, no two marine worms are exactly the same. Some marine worms are considered 'free-living' because they have bristles all along their bodies that they use to wriggle through the water in a snakelike way. Others are bottom-dwellers that find a spot on the ocean floor and stay there for long periods of time, using their long tentacles to catch plankton.

X

XANTHID CRAB

Habitat: Warm, coastal areas

Size: Up to 10 centimetres wide

Diet: Plants and algae

Crabs belonging to the Xanthidae family have black-tipped claws and are deadly to eat. Unlike jellyfish or lionfish, these toxic crabs have no way of injecting their poison into their prey, so poisoning only occurs when they are eaten. The poison in their muscles is so powerful that even a small mouthful is enough to kill a human!

X-RAY TETRA

Habitat: Rivers and estuaries

Size: Up to 5 centimetres long

Diet: Worms, crustaceans and insects

With its translucent skin and visible skeleton, the X-ray tetra's name is very fitting. Not only does an X-ray tetra's skin shimmer when it swims, its see-through skin also helps it hide from predators. These fish also have strong hearing abilities thanks to their skeleton, which picks up sound waves and helps them find the nearest source of food! These fish usually live in South American rivers, but they are able to cope with salty water and are sometimes found in estuaries, where rivers meet the sea.

Y

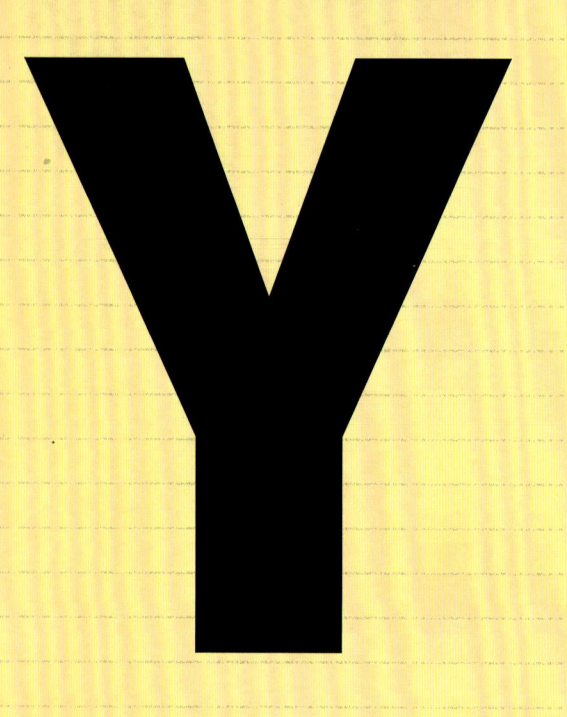

YELLOW-BELLIED SEA SNAKE

Habitat: Open ocean
Size: Up to 1.5 metres long
Diet: Fish

Most sea snakes tend to live close to coasts, but the yellow-bellied sea snake is one of few open-ocean sea snakes. They live in the Pacific Ocean, often in large groups. Yellow-bellied sea snakes have deadly venom in their fangs that they use to paralyze their prey.

YELLOWFIN TUNA

Habitat: Warm, open ocean

Size: Up to 2.1 metres long

Diet: Mostly fish and squid

True to their name, these large, fast-swimming fish have bright-yellow fins that make them easily recognizable. Yellowfin tuna live in the Pacific, Atlantic and Indian Oceans, and they often swim in large groups with other tuna or even dolphins! These fish are one of the ocean's top predators and help maintain balance in their ecosystems.

Z

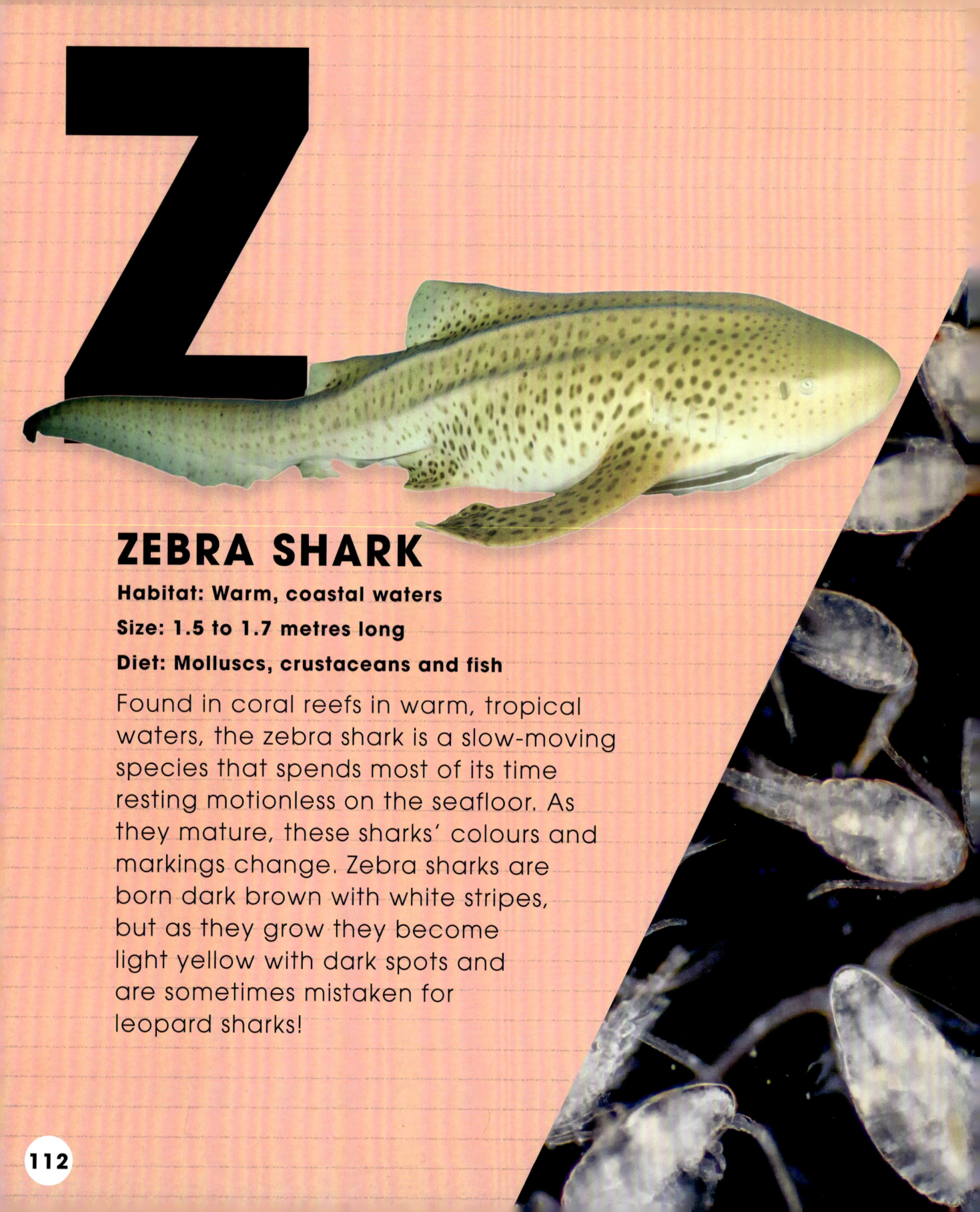

ZEBRA SHARK

Habitat: Warm, coastal waters
Size: 1.5 to 1.7 metres long
Diet: Molluscs, crustaceans and fish

Found in coral reefs in warm, tropical waters, the zebra shark is a slow-moving species that spends most of its time resting motionless on the seafloor. As they mature, these sharks' colours and markings change. Zebra sharks are born dark brown with white stripes, but as they grow they become light yellow with dark spots and are sometimes mistaken for leopard sharks!

ZOOPLANKTON

Habitat: Open ocean and coastal areas
Size: Microscopic to 20 centimetres long
Diet: Plankton, especially algae

There are millions of small organisms that drift along with the ocean's currents, many of which are zooplankton. Some zooplankton stay small, while other plankton will eventually mature to be larger animals, such as starfish, clams and other bottom-dwellers.

ZOOXANTHELLAE

Habitat: Corals and giant clams
Size: Microscopic
Diet: Sunlight

Small green algae that live in corals and giant clams are called zooxanthellae (pronounced zoo-zan-thell-ee). They need sunlight to live because they use the Sun's energy to turn carbon dioxide and water into food and oxygen. Many sea creatures rely on these tiny, plantlike organisms to survive and in return, the zooxanthellae are given a safe place to live!

Z

ZONES

The ocean can be divided into habitats called zones. Each zone has different conditions, so different types of animals live there, although some animals have adapted to move between zones.

- Sunlight zone
- Twilight zone
- Midnight zone
- Abyssal zone

Sunlight Zone

Sunlight passes through the top 200 metres of the ocean, which is called the sunlight zone. Small invertebrates, such as plankton, live in the sunlight zone. Fish and other animals live in this zone too, and feed on the plankton. Most marine animals that need to come to the surface to breathe spend their lives in the sunlight zone.

Twilight Zone

At depths of 200 to 1000 metres, there is very little light. The water is colder, and there is less food for animals to eat. This is called the twilight zone.

Midnight Zone

Below 1000 metres, there is no sunlight at all, so this is called the midnight zone. There are no plants or algae in the midnight zone, so food is hard to find. The animals that live here survive in complete darkness, except for any bioluminescent light they make themselves.

Abyssal Zone

The abyssal zone is the largest zone of the ocean, covering 300 million square kilometres. At depths greater than 2000 metres, this zone is extremely cold and includes the seafloor, which can be rocky, sandy, or muddy. This is an enormous ocean habitat that provides food and shelter for many animals.

A B C
G H I
M N O
S T U V

D E F
J K L
P Q R
W X Y Z

117

GLOSSARY

Bioluminescence: the shining of light from a living creature

Cartilage: a tough, flexible material

Cnidarians: invertebrate marine animals with tentacles, such as corals, anemones and jellyfish

Cold-blooded: having a body temperature that changes depending on the surroundings

Conservation: planned management of natural resources to prevent destruction of habitats or extinction

Echolocation: a method dolphins, and some whales, use to find objects using sound waves

Exoskeleton: the strong shell-like skin on some types of invertebrates, e.g. crustaceans

Extinct: no longer living

Habitat: a place where plants or animals naturally live

Mammals: animals that are warm-blooded, covered in hair, and give birth to live young

Mantle: the soft, muscular tissue covering a mollusc's body

Photosynthesis: the process in which green plants use sunlight to turn water and carbon dioxide into food

Species: a category of related living things

Symbiotic: when two distinct organisms live together and benefit each other

Warm-blooded: having a body temperature that stays the same no matter the surroundings

119

Picture Credits

t = top, b = bottom, l = left, r = right, c = centre

age Fotostock
100–101 Steve Downer/ardea

Alamy
15 Solvin Zankl, 21bc Melba Photo Agency, 25 Frank Hecker, 28t Solvin Zankl/Nature Picture Library, 34tl David Shale/Nature Picture Library, 62 dotted zebra, 89 background Frank Hecker

Getty
10–11 Matjaz Slanic, 60–61 Michael Nolan, 74c _548901005677, 75bl James R.D. Scott, 80–81 Mint Images

Nature Picture Library
16–17 Alex Mustard, 70tl Georgette Douwma, 87bl Nick Upton, 103 Martin Gabriel

Science Photo Library
43 Solvin Zankl/Nature Picture Library, 55 Jany Sauvanet, 87tr Georgette Douwma

Shutterstock
Front cover tr Vladmir Melnik, c bluehand, b Kletr, bl bluehand, 3, 106 Fata Morgana by Andrew Marriott, 4–5, 90–91 Shane Myers Photography, 6–7 Wild_and_free_naturephoto, 8–9 Regina Bilan, 12 Anton Rodionov, 13 Andrew Burgess, 13, 88 background Richard Whitcombe, 14 Anake Seenadee, 18–19b Carlos Aguilera, 19tr Johannes Kornelius, 20 arka38, 21t Jazmine Thomas, bl Ethan Daniels, br Palo_ok, background Damsea, 22–23 Imagine Earth Photography, 24 Dr Norbert Lange, 26–27 Tory Kallman, 28c Frolova_Elena, 28b Neil Bromhall, 29t Konstantin Novikov, 29b superjoseph, 30tl ChristianChan, 30–31 Picture Partners, 32l Kotomiti Okuma, 32–33 Danita Delmont, 34–35 aquapix, 35br COZ, 36–37 Damsea, 38bl David A. Litman, 38–39t Andrea Izzotti, 39tr Alexandre Ornellas, 40tl Kletr, 40–41b Tomas Kotouc, 42 pawanya phatarakulkajorn, 44–45 background Damsea, 45b Eddie Cheever, 46l Butterfly Hunter, 46–47 Jazmine Thomas, 48–49 Kerimli, 50 Daniel Poloha, 51 Tory Kallman, 52 Ben Queenborough, 53 background Andrea Izzotti, 53r RLS photo, 54 Marben, 56 Erika Kirkpatrick, 56–57 Irina_Kulikova, 58tl Damsea, 58–59t Kjersti Joergensen, 59br Jiang Hongyan, 61tr Emily-Cross, 61br vkilikov, 63 bluehand, 64 MyImages - Micha, 65 Kondratuk Aleksei, 66 worldswildlifewonders, 67 Neil Burton, 68–69 Rich Carey, 70–71b Alexey Seafarer, 71tr Ivanne, 72 eshoot, 73 Beth Swanson, 74b divedog, 75tr D.J. Schuessler Jr, 76 Danita Delmont, 77 Armin Rose, 78 chonlasub woravichan, 79 Becky Gill, 82 Tracey Winholt, 83 Janos Rautonen, 84b fivespots, 84–85t, 85tr Rich Carey, 85b Johann Helgason, 86 Leah-Anne Thompson, 88 GOLFX, 89 Levent Konuk, 92t Dr Ajay Kumar Singh, 92b Russell Watkins, 93t Alexey Seafarer, 93b Harry Turner, 94–95 Rich Carey, 96 NancyRutlege, 97 Vlad61, 98 Laura Dinraths, 99 Damsea, 102 Takayuki Ohama, 104t Christopher Wood, 105b OHishiapply, 107 Rich Carey, 108 davemhuntphotography, 109 Andrew Williams, 110 Ken Griffiths, 111 Shane Gross, 112l Rich Carey, 112–113 Choksawatdikorn, 113r bearacreative, 114 NoPainNoGain, 118–119 Pearawas Tangjitaurboon, cover spine Konstantin G, back cover tl Anton Rodionov, br dive-hive, bl chonlasub woravichan

The author/editor and publisher gratefully acknowledge the permission granted to reproduce the copyright material in this book. Every effort has been made to trace copyright holders and to obtain their permission for the use of copyright material. The publisher apologizes for any errors or omissions in the above list and would be grateful if notified of any corrections that should be incorporated in future reprints or editions of this book.